DOVER GAME AND PUZZLE ACTIVITY BOOKS

Sports Mazes

DAVE PHILLIPS

DOVER PUBLICATIONS, INC.
New York

DOVER GAME AND PUZZLE ACTIVITY BOOKS

Bibliographical Note

Sports Mazes is a new work, first published by Dover Publications, Inc., in 1994.

International Standard Book Number: 0-486-28277-5

Manufactured in the United States of America
Dover Publications, Inc., 31 East 2nd Street, Mineola, N.Y. 11501

Note

THE THEME OF this new collection of mazes by mazemaster Dave Phillips is sports—almost any kind you can think of. As in the sports themselves, you must follow the rules, so carefully read the instructions with each maze. The first mazes are the easiest, later ones more of a challenge. Do well, and you'll soon be ready for the maze Olympics!

SAILING

Enter the maze, pass through all sailboats, then exit the maze without using any path more than once.

RUNNING

Enter the maze, pass through all runners, then exit the maze without using any path more than once.

FOOTBALL

Enter the maze, pass through all footballs, then exit the maze without using any path more than once.

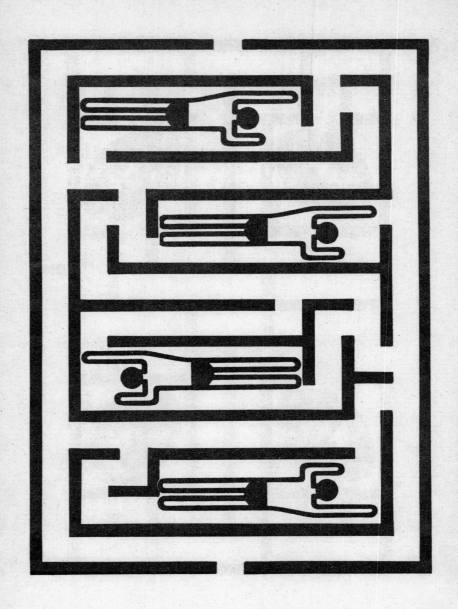

SWIMMING
Enter the maze, pass through all swimmers, then exit the maze without using any path more than once.

BALLOONING

Enter the maze, pass through all balloons, then exit the maze without using any path more than once.

5

CAR RACING

Enter the maze, pass through all cars, then exit the maze without using any path more than once.

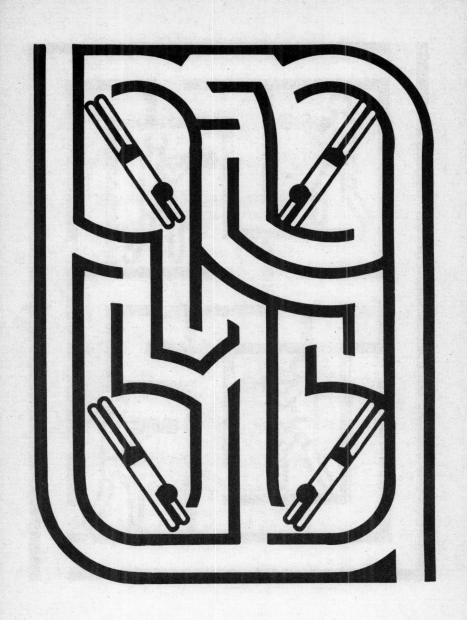

DIVING

Enter the maze, pass through all divers, then exit the maze without using any path more than once.

BOXING

Enter the maze, pass through all boxers, then exit the maze without using any path more than once.

LUGE

Enter the maze, pass through all lugers, then exit the maze without using any path more than once.

CROSS-COUNTRY SKIING

Enter the maze, pass through all skiers, then exit the maze without using any path more than once.

HORSE RACING

Enter the maze, pass through all horses, then exit the maze without using any path more than once.

11

SCUBA DIVING

Enter the maze, pass through all scuba divers, then exit the maze without using any path more than once.

FENCING

Enter the maze, pass through all fencers, then exit the maze without using any path more than once.

13

GYMNASTICS

Enter the maze, pass through all gymnasts, then exit the maze without using any path more than once.

HANG GLIDING

Enter the maze, pass through all hang gliders, then exit the maze without using any path more than once.

15

FIGURE SKATING

Enter the maze, pass through all figure skaters, then exit the maze without using any path more than once.

16

SURFING

Enter the maze, pass through all surfers, then exit the maze without using any path more than once.

CABER TOSSING

Enter the maze, pass through all caber tossers, then exit the maze without using any path more than once.

SKATEBOARDING

Enter the maze, pass through both skateboards, the pads and the helmet (not necessarily in that order), then exit the maze without using any path more than once.

STEEPLECHASING

Enter the maze, pass through all obstacles, then exit the maze without using any path more than once.

CYCLING

Enter the maze, pass through all cyclists, then exit the maze without using any path more than once.

SPEED SKATING
Enter the maze, pass through all speed skaters, then exit the maze without using any path more than once.

GOLF

Enter the maze, pass through all holes, then exit the maze without using any path more than once.

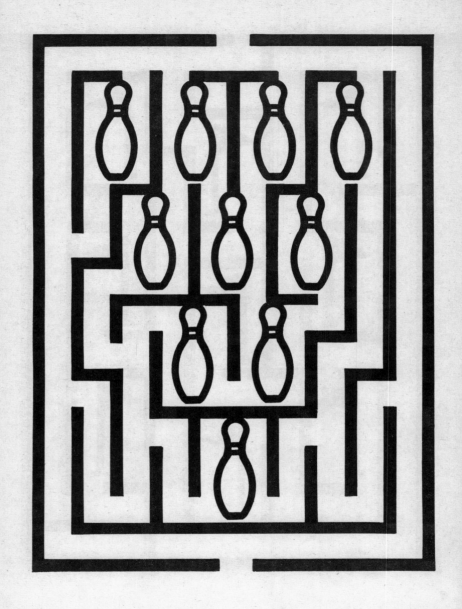

BOWLING

Enter the maze, pass through all pins, then exit the maze without using any path more than once.

ARCHERY

Enter the maze, pass through all arrows and the target, then exit the maze without using any path more than once. You must pass through the target last.

WEIGHT LIFTING

Enter the maze, pass through all weights, then exit the maze without using any path more than once. You must pass through the largest weight last.

DARTS

Enter the maze, pass through all darts and the target, then exit the maze without using any path more than once. You must pass through the target last.

FISHING

Enter the maze, pass through the fish and the flies, then exit the maze without using any path more than once. You must go to a fish from a fly.

ICE HOCKEY

Enter the maze, pass through the sticks and the pucks, then exit
the maze without using any path more than once. You must go to a
puck from a stick.

LACROSSE

Enter the maze, pass through the sticks and the balls, then exit the maze without using any path more than once. You must go to a ball from a stick.

SOCCER

Enter the maze, pass through the balls and the goals, then exit the maze without using any path more than once. You must go to a goal from a ball.

PING-PONG

Enter the maze, pass through all paddles and balls, then exit the maze without using any path more than once. You must go to a paddle from a ball.

HORSESHOES

Enter the maze, pass through all shoes and posts, then exit the maze without using any path more than once. You must go to a post from a shoe.

BASKETBALL

Enter the maze, pass through all hoops and balls, then exit the maze without using any path more than once. You must go to a hoop from a ball.

CROQUET

Enter the maze, pass through all hoops and balls, then exit the maze without using any path more than once. You must go to a hoop from a ball.

VOLLEYBALL

Enter the maze, pass through all balls, then exit the maze without using any path more than once. You must cross the net without crossing your path after each ball.

TENNIS

Enter the maze, pass through all rackets, then exit the maze without using any path more than once. You must cross the net without crossing your path after each racket.

CRICKET

Enter the maze, pass through all bats, wickets and balls, then exit the maze without using any path more than once. You must use the order of ball to bat to wicket.

BASEBALL

Enter the maze, pass through all bats, gloves and balls, then exit the maze without using any path more than once. You must use the order of bat to ball to glove.

POOL

Enter the maze, pass through all balls, then exit the maze without using any path more than once. You must pass through the balls in numerical order.

Solutions

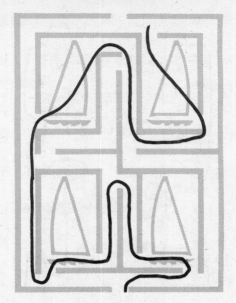

Sailing, *page 1*

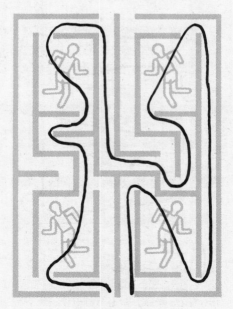

Running, *page 2*

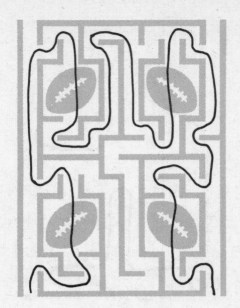

Football, *page 3*

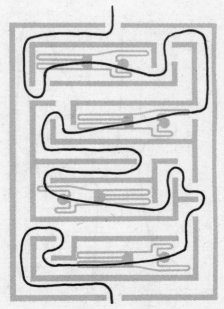

Swimming, *page 4*

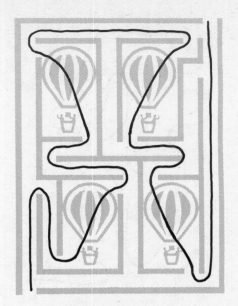

Ballooning, *page 5*

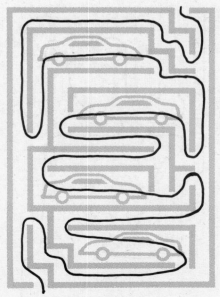

Car Racing, *page 6*

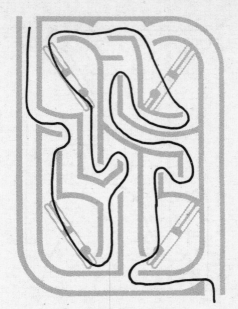

Diving, *page 7*

Boxing, *page 8*

Luge, *page 9*

Cross-Country Skiing, *page 10*

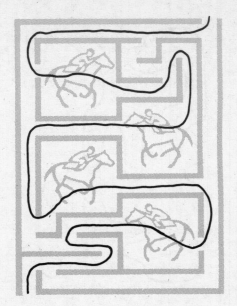

Horse Racing, *page 11*

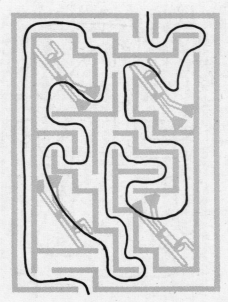

Scuba Diving, *page 12*

Fencing, *page 13*

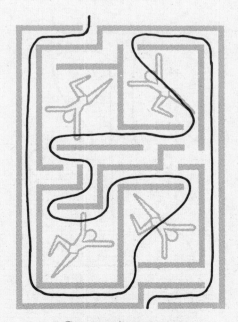

Gymnastics, *page 14*

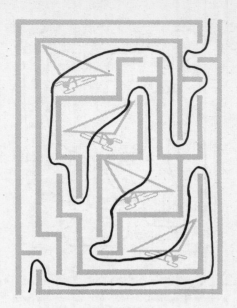

Hang Gliding, *page 15*

Figure Skating, *page 16*

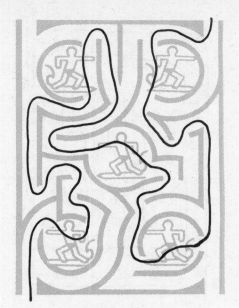

Surfing, *page 17*

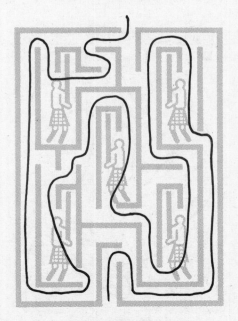

Caber Tossing, *page 18*

49

Skateboarding, *page 19*

Steeplechasing, *page 20*

Cycling, *page 21*

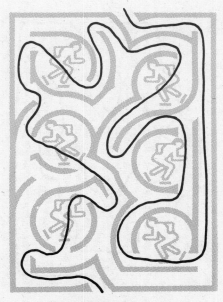

Speed Skating, *page 22*

51

Golf, *page 23*

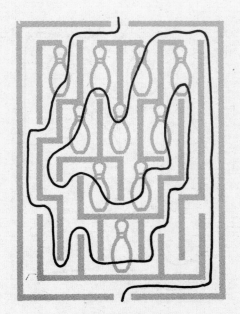

Bowling, *page 24*

Archery, *page 25*

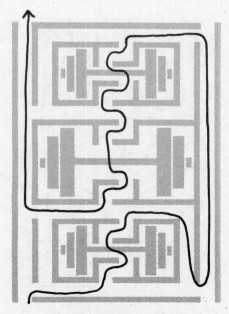

Weight Lifting, *page 26*

53

Darts, *page 27*

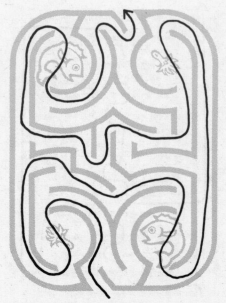

Fishing, *page 28*

Ice Hockey, *page 29*

Lacrosse, *page 30*

Soccer, *page 31*

Ping-Pong, *page 32*

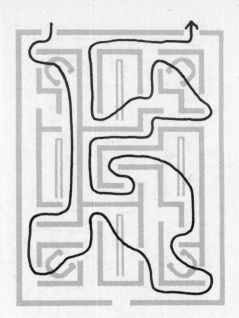

Horseshoes, *page 33*

Basketball, *page 34*

Croquet, *page 35*

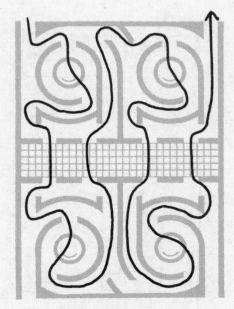

Volleyball, *page 36*